HOUSE OF ABBAS

THE LEGACY OF HARUN AL-RASHID

HOUSE OF ABBAS

THE LEGACY OF HARUN AL-RASHID

ALI TELMESANI

CLARITAS
BOOKS

1 2 3 4 5 6 7 8 9 10

CLARITAS BOOKS

Bernard Street, Swansea, United Kingdom
Milpitas, California, United States

First Published in August 2018

Typeset in Minion Pro 14/11
Printed by Mega Printing in Turkey

House of Abbas: The Legacy of Harun al-Rashid
By Ali Telmesani

A CIP catalogue record for this book is available from the British Library

ISBN 978-1-905837-52-6

Ali Telmesani is a poet, playwright, songwriter and filmmaker. Ali formally began studying creative writing during his Undergraduate studies in English Literature at the University of Connecticut. Having developed a keen interest in Islamic philosophy, Sufi metaphysics and literature, Ali completed an MA in Islamic Studies at Claremont Graduate University in Southern California before earning his second MA in Creative Writing at Swansea University in South Wales. Along with producing a collection of short stories for his creative thesis, Ali has published several poems in literary journals and founded his own, The Gull, with a colleague at Swansea University. In between his studies, he pursued a career as a composer and musician in Amherst, Massachusetts. Most recently, Ali founded Whetstone Center for the Arts in Jeddah, KSA, where he teaches music and creative writing.

CONTENTS

FORWEORD

I would like to begin by discussing briefly the complexities of recounting Islamic history and Islamic figures, particularly the Caliphs, or as they are referred to in Islamdom - the Commanders of the Faithful. As is the case with the annals of Western history, it is always the victors that write them. The recounting of Islamic history by Muslim historians - all throughout the Medieval period, up to the establishment of the modern Academy in the 20th century - is no exception.

It is quite typical throughout the Islamic world that discussions of its history is always a touchy subject. Predictably, sectarian factionalism plays a strong role in this touchiness. There is no such thing as a cohesive, uniform recollection of Islamic history. As it was in the time of the subjects of this play in the 9th Century CE, it always depends on where you come from in the Islamic world. This touchiness is also exasperated by a desire by

Muslims to project a positive image of Islam's overarching history to the rest of the world, and preventing that image from being tainted by the inevitably ugly realities that are an integrated part of human history itself. It is important to note that this form of projection is how every person, from every corner of the world, would like to remember their own history - British colonists never gathered round a table with Native Americans to give thanks, break bread and eat corn and turkey with their 'beloved' new neighbours, yet that is how American families prefer to recall what was actually a brutal and bloody history to their children (at least, this was the case with this American until he reached high school).

I would like to propose the notion that the true beauty of history is the fact that it contains both the ugly and the beautiful, the dark and the hopeful, the ruthless and the beneficent. History in this sense should be appreciated the same way brilliant art should be appreciated. No expression of art that expressed itself in a sterile and rosy way ever stood the test of time. We still read John Milton's Paradise Lost because it is almost as disturbing and thought-provoking as it was when published in the 17th Century. Entwined with the sheer deft and brilliance of Milton's lyricism, it makes Paradise Lost all the more devastating and profound in its impact on us as a product of intrinsic 'Beauty'. There should be no difference in the way we appreciate our own history. What makes it beautiful is that it portrays the very spectrum of the human condition.

The figure of the Abbasid Caliph Harun al-Rashid (d. 809 CE), who ruled at the peak of the Islamic Golden Age, is best known in the West by virtue of The Book of One Thousand and One Nights (alf layla wa layla), whose setting takes place in his Caliphal court in Baghdad. Despite the setting, Harun al-Rashid figures only in some of its tales.

Harun al-Rashid remains a notorious figure in the annals of Islamic history. A healthy majority of Muslims revere him as the greatest of all Caliphs due to his presiding over an Islamic empire in its Golden Age - a prolific period of scientific, religious and artistic prosperity and innovation. His notoriety, however, is also marked by his ruthlessness towards his milk brother and vizir, Yahya al-Barmaki, whose family of Barmakids played a major role in establishing the Abbasid Caliphate. The downfall of the Khurasani (Persian) Barmakids at the hands of Harun al-Rashid has proved to be a stain on al-Rashid's rule. This Arab/Persian falling out is echoed in the unfortunate modern manifestations of geopolitical hostility between Arab and Persian powers to this day.

The historical figure of Harun al-Rashid does not differ greatly from the romanticised figure that features in The Book of One Thousand and One Nights. Medieval Muslim historians offer plenty of laudatory descriptions of a Caliph whom they say, for example, prayed one hundred prostrations a day and donated daily 1,000 dirhams to charitable causes from his own coffers. On the other hand, his reputation suffered dearly from his alleged courtly ostentatiousness, bacchanals, lavish banquets and unbridled generosity towards poets, ascetics and favoured courtesans. Nonetheless, the figure of Harun al-Rashid has survived generally as a positive character, if not a deeply revered and idolised Caliph in the long history of Caliphs throughout Islamic history.

The main characters in this play are two of Harun al-Rashid's sons. The first, Muhammad ibn Harun al-Rashid (d. 813 CE), is known by the regnal name of al-Amin - born of Harun and his only queen, Zubayda, who also features in the play. The second is al-Amin's half-brother Abul Abbas al-Ma'mun ibn Harun al-Rashid (d. 833 CE) - simply known as al-Ma'mun - who was born of Harun al-Rashid and a Persian concubine whose name is unknown to us. Though the half-brother is older than al-Amin, it is the latter who was bound, and indeed succeeded their father as Caliph due to his purely royal bloodline. Both figures remain as notorious in the history books as their father in their own right.

Al-Amin is remembered in the histories as the perpetrator of the civil war between himself and his brother, but whose actual role in starting the civil war is questionable. On the other hand, al-Ma'mun is remembered in the histories primarily as the initiator of the Mihna - a campaign of religious persecution towards religious scholars who opposed the Mu'tazilite doctrine of the createdness of the Qur'an. Their doctrine goes against the overwhelmingly orthodox view that the Qur'an is uncreated, that it is an eternally and preternally preserved tablet (al-Lawh al-Mahfuz) of pure divine revelation. It is because of these monumental moments in the brothers' personal histories that Muslims prefer to look back upon their father, Harun a-Rashid, as the apogee and bezel of the Abbasid Caliphate during its most prosperous period - the calm before the storm, if you will.

Harun al-Rashid was plagued by the prospect of having his son al-Amin succeed him as Caliph due to his hedonistic proclivities and lack of care for serious study or stately duties. In his adolescence, he did not seem to grasp the daunting spectre of advancing or even maintaining the interests of his father's vast empire, soon to be past down to him. This was apparent to Harun from the very early stages of al-Amin's youth. In contrast, al-Ma'mun was a serious man of learning, who excelled in his studies and bore the burden of responsibility and expectation as the second in line to the throne. Al-Ma'mun was more than happy to surround himself with the finest scientists, astrologers and Mu'tazilite scholars the son of the Caliph could be afforded. He had a particular penchant for Greek philosophy, was an ardent student of

Aristotelianism and never hesitated to challenge the hadith literature in favour of logic and rationalism. Along with his mature demeanor and respect for the office his father held, it made Harun al-Rashid all the more anxious that it was the younger, more reckless al-Amin who would succeed him. Nonetheless, Zubayda, the empress and mother of al-Amin, found it inconceivable that al-Ma'mun - the son of a concubine - would ever be placed before her son, no matter how intensely her husband pressed her. She simply turned a blind eye to her son's flaws and pushed for al-Amin to succeed her husband.

It is important to note the difference between history, as was recorded by medieval and modern historians, and historiography - the study of how history was written. As aforementioned, history is recorded by the victors, and it would be ridiculous to assume that any historian was bereft of predisposition or prejudice. There is a plethora of historical writings by medieval and modern writers of Islamic history, as well as hagiographical sources that paint these characters in every light and color. Therefore, it is impossible to verify the historicity of any and all accounts of Harun and his sons. This leaves the study of Islamic historiography as the only hope for those bent on understanding what may or may not be historically veracious. In the end, it is a matter of engaging in as much historiographical research as possible and deciding for oneself what may or may not have actually taken place.

While undertaking my own historiographical research, my interest was in studying the most sober and fantastical depictions of al-Amin and al-Ma'mun from the historical and hagiographical accounts related to these figures for the sole purpose of telling a good story. My research bore what was to me a drama - a bona fide tragedy - that was truly Shakespearean in scope. In composing this work, I had no intention whatsoever in portraying historically accurate depictions of the figures featured in this work. Ultimately, this play, this dramatic poem, is an expression of art. It is pure historical fiction. Nothing more, nothing less.

Amman, Jordan
July 7th, 2018

DRAMATIS PERSONÆ

Muhammad al-Amīn	Son of Hārūn al-Rashīd and Queen Zubayda, al-Ma'mūn's half-brother
Abul Abbas al-Ma'mūn	Son of Hārūn al-Rashīd and a Persian concubine, al-Amīn's half-brother
Zubayda	Wife of Hārūn al-Rashīd, al-Amīn's mother
Waliyyah	Caliphal servant
Wazir	Advisor to the caliphs Hārūn al-Rashīd and al-Amīn

ACT I, SCENE I

The caliphal court. Waliyyah, cleaning a window, stops to stare out upon Baghdad

Waliyyah

Baghdad. My Baghdad. The jewel, the envy
of the world.

Turns to address the audience

I watched it grow from what was nothing. I witnessed it from the inside out, lived to serve its architect, the great caliph, Hārūn al-Rashīd, the Rightly Guided. It was an enchanting time. I beheld many marvels. Baghdad– the jewel, the envy of the world; the center of learning, the haven of arts and culture. The most eager minds flocked from the farthest corners of the earth to taste of its fruit, drink of its fountains; for a chance to sit at the feet of the most brilliant minds the world has ever seen. In this very court, I've witnessed extraordinary men of philosophy and science, the finest musicians and silver-tongued poets who'd rival the constellations in their magnanimity. Indeed, God bestowed a hallowed light upon my caliph, who likewise reflected it upon his people. To serve his blessed hands was an honour beyond compare, unfit for a lowly servant such as I. But all great kings must make way for the next. It became my charge to raise the sons of al-Rashid, the future caliphs of this vast empire.

Prepares a vessel of wine, returns to the window, looks back out onto the city

Baghdad. Oh, Baghdad I feel the winds of changing shift. May God most High maintain our blessed city in what's to come. I pray that, by serving its new custodian, I continue to serve her too.

The caliph al-Amīn enters stage left, sits upon his throne

al-Amīn

Waliyyah, please, bring me some wine if you will.

Waliyyah, unresponsive, continues to stare out the window

Waliyyah, did you not hear me? Bring me wine!
What is it that captures your attention so?

Waliyyah
Forgive me, oh Commander of the Faithful.
I was merely marveling at your capitol.

Waliyyah brings him wine

al-Amīn
Does it not belong to you as well,
my dear Waliyyah?

Waliyyah
It is I that belongs to her, my lord,
as I belong to her sovereign.

al-Amīn
It has changed since my father's time,
has it not?

Waliyyah
Only for the better, my caliph.

al-Amīn
Perhaps it is the lens with which we look
upon it that has changed, for surely this

is not my father's court.

Waliyyah
If I may speak freely, my lord…

al-Amīn
You may.

Waliyyah
...your father, whom I was blessed to have served, no doubt
was a noble and accomplished ruler, but now
it is time for you to carry on beyond
his vision– to create your own.

al-Amīn
Yes, yes. Vision.

quaffs his wine and gestures for another

There will be time for that. What is that verse?
God is with those who are patient?

Wazir, side stage, awaits permission to enter

Wazir
My lord?

al-Amīn
Ah! Speaking of vision… come in my Wazir.
What news have you for me today?

Wazir
It is your brother, my caliph. He's just arrived
from Persia.

al-Amīn
Strange. Why was I not notified
ahead of time?

Wazir
There was no notification received, my lord.
From his demeanor, he seems to be in some
consternation.

al-Amīn
How surprising.

al-Amīn takes another drink. Enter al-Ma'mūn

al-Amīn
Ah, here he is! Arrived at last,
all the way from Marv. The indomitable
al-Ma'mūn. You grace us all with your presence.
Come come, brother, have a drink with me.

Waliyyah! Another glass! Come on Ma'mun,
caliph's orders. That will be all, Wazir.
The governor of Persia and I, we have some catching
up to do.

Wazir bows his head and takes his leave.

al-Ma'mūn
Thank you dear brother. Good to see you as always.

al-Amīn
What are you waiting for, join me will you?

Waliyyah offers al-Ma'mūn a glass of wine

al-Ma'mūn
No thank you, Waliyyah my dear. Muhammad, you know
I do not drink. Anyway, it seems you've had
more than your fill. I'd hate to overindulge
My commander.

al-Amīn
Well then, if you'd deny me a wine-partner,
then let me fill your belly with Baghdad's finest.
Waliyyah!

al-Ma'mūn
Thank you, brother, but there are pressing affairs
of state to address.

al-Amīn
Tell me then. What brings you back from Marv?
I pray your journey this time was manageable?
Those steppes… they are dreadful in the wintertime.

al-Ma'mūn
The journey was fair dear brother. But please I must
insist…

al-Amīn
Go on, spit it out.

al-Ma'mūn
Muhammad, please. Have you not received the official
papers I sent through my courier? They'd been…
accumulating. I sent them weeks ago!
Your entire army hasn't been paid in months,
there are cases to survey and punishments to be meted out,
not to mention that minor little thing
called legislature. Those need ratification
as soon as possible! My courier tells me you've
received the stack, all of it.

al-Amīn
Ah, yes. That old thing.

Points to the pile

al-Ma'mūn
Have you not looked at them?

al-Amīn
Now who said that? Of course I've looked at them.
I've perused, inspected, examined, waded through…
A dozen pages in though, my God was I bored!
A busy bee still needs his break. Don't worry.
Trust, brother. My intentions are steadfast.
Remember brother, God is with the patient.

Downs his glass

al-Ma'mūn
The only thing steadfast is that liver of yours.
Does it not need a busy break as well?

al-Amīn
Mind your manners governor. Waliyyah!
Papers!

He flips through a few of them, signing them hurriedly

al-Ma'mūn
This title is not a game, Muhammad. It requires
constant attention. It's not a pleasure boat
for you to wallow on to pass the time.
Or do your Persian provinces matter not?

al-Amīn
Is that not why I made you governor there
brother? Are you not kin to them, Persian?

al-Ma'mūn
Do you not share a father with this Persian?
or do you mock his honour too? For shame,
little brother. Tell me, where lies your dignity?

al-Amīn
Mine was bestowed, big brother, by
our noble father and his nobler queen
the mother of the believers of Islam. Where is yours
again exactly?

al-Ma'mūn
Careful little brother.

al-Amīn
Come on, brother, enough of this bickering
of status, who is legitimate and who is not.

Aren't we all legitimate in the eyes of God,
the Lord of the Worlds? The One who matters most?
I am but the lord of this one. And you
of Persia, that fertile realm you love so well.
Has my appointment not fully satisfied?
What else do you need? Gold? Women? A Harem?

al-Ma'mūn
A Leader. A Caliph. A Commander. A head of state.
It's not just me, Muhammad. Your people. Our people.

al-Amīn
My people!

He picks up and pours the rest of his jug of wine over the rest of the pile, smiling

There's your damn legislature.
My, my. That was hard work, wasn't it?
Waliyyah! Burn this pile of nonsense! And wine!
More!

As Waliyyah leaves, al-Ma'mūn storms off. al-Amīn downs another glass.

al-Amīn
Ungrateful. Greedy! I've given him everything,

and what does he come here for? Legislature!
Does he fancy me his personal secretary?
Legislature. The nerve. Act like a brother,
respect me like one! Not that I need respect
from some half-Persian illegitimate son
of a concubine. Have I not treated him, loved him
As my own? Our father afforded us
the finest education on God's green earth,
fed us literature, arithmetic, *phi-lo-so-phy*...
Aristotle this, Plato that...
Pah! More than he deserves.

Waliyyah returns with more wine.

Waliyyah
The empress, my lord.

Zubayda enters

Zubayda
That will be all, Waliyyah. Now run along.

Waliyyah exits

My darling son, apple of my eye.
Tell me what troubles the caliph, lord of the land?

al-Amīn
Ma'mun...

quaffs his drink

he insults me, my leadership.
Fancies himself a wise man, a jurist, a pedant.
Fancies himself to be our father. Another
al-Rashid. He tries so hard. He tries
in desperate hopes of feeling powerful.
Did I not make him the sovereign of all of Persia?
How much more can a younger brother care
for his elder sibling?

Zubayda
Half-sibling.

al-Amīn
Half-sibling or not, deep down I know, father
favoured him as his successor. Don't you
tell me otherwise.

Zubayda
Stop! You stop right now! *You*
are the rightful heir to this empire, God's
vicegerent on this earth! *You* are the son,
the *legitimate* son of Harun and his queen! Me!

Zubayda! Mother of all believers! and no-one.
No-one can prevent you from your divine
inheritance, least of whom your father!
Now. If you fret about your brother, you fret
in vain, my precious. He is simply jealous–
jealous of his lot. Leave him be.
He cannot cheat fate and neither can you.
What you need is to sit back and relax.
Waliyyah! More wine!

Waliyyah enters with another flagon

and send for the concubines.
Our dearest caliph needs unwinding.

END SCENE

ACT I, SCENE II

al-Ma'mūn alone late at night in the caliphal court

al-Ma'mūn
What *is* it that you crave? Infernal throne!
of silver, gold, jewels, dead animal hide
surrounded by walls in an empty palace hall...
were you meant for miserly, gluttonous aristocrats?
Tyrant noblemen, noble tyrants? Frauds?!
Were you not built by tired, modest hands?
Oh how do inanimate things represent empires
of smiths, cobblers, bakers and artisans?
Where is your pauper philosopher king
who's envy is the meek, downtrodden soul?
Where is your champion of God's dominion,
true in faith, steadfast in will, magnanimous
at heart, the lion *and* the lamb? Tell me,
where is your intellectual steward

well-versed in poetry, music, art and calligraphy?
Our culture needs a vulnerable soul to survive!
Of course… ruthlessness also has its place.
Against the enemy, one must be clinical.
But don't we also deserve a politician
In times peace? Ha! Peace. Of which
he'll never know! His armies are disaffected,
yet to be paid; riots and rebellions brew,
enemies loom nigh.

the door crashes open, al-Amīn barges in followed by Zubayda and Waliyyah

al-Amīn

Insolent, condescending, backbiting cretins!
They patronize *me*, their supreme commander, their caliph?

Zubayda

Muhammad, they are your council. It's what they do!

al-Amīn

Every one of them, I should have their heads!

Zubayda

Calm down Muhammad, you cannot kill them all!

al-Amīn
And why not, *mother?* They jump to criticize
my judgment, my actions? Who are *they* to speak?
Lost in their antiquated theologies?
This is *my* dominion– *I* maintain this world,
Not God.

Zubayda
Careful Muhammad.

al-Amīn
And what are *you* looking at?

finally noticing al-Ma'mūn's presence

does something amuse you?

al-Ma'mūn
Nothing my commander.

al-Amīn
Oh save your petty formalities. I've had
enough patronising to last me a lifetime.

al-Ma'mūn
Are they not your jurists? Your councilmen?
They only advise you out of concern.

al-Amīn
Well they should be concerned about their own pathetic well-being. Oh yes, they'll earn their wages.

Zubayda
Muhammad!

al-Amīn storms off, followed by Zubayda

al-Ma'mūn
Wait! Waliyyah don't go.

Waliyyah
but…

al-Ma'mūn
Please. Please stay.

al-Ma'mūn reaches out, she holds him

Waliyyah
Habibi, my dear sweet boy.

al-Ma'mūn
How are you?

Waliyyah
I'm fine.

al-Ma'mūn
How are you, *really*?

Waliyyah
Well… it's not the same as it used to be.

al-Ma'mūn
Does he treat you well?

Waliyyah
Of course he does. I raised the boy, didn't I?
The both of you.

al-Ma'mūn
It didn't look like it that day I arrived.

Waliyyah
He was just drunk. Don't you worry. He wouldn't
dare try crossing me. I know the boy
infinitely better than his own mother.

al-Ma'mūn
You were our mother. You know that.

Waliyyah
And you were my little boys. Devils really.

al-Ma'mūn
... I miss father. Deeply. Especially now.
Oh if he were here. I miss you too
of course. I cannot stand how far away
you are from me. It feels like he's banished me there
in Persia... thinks he's done me some kind of favour.

Waliyyah
I think I know, my dear, who you miss.

al-Ma'mūn
I don't even recognise him anymore!
Every time I see him I just feel sick!
My little brother. Gone! God it hurts!
What pangs are these Waliyyah? An orphan boy
wrenched away, away without a home!

Waliyyah
Habibi, this is your home. Always.

al-Ma'mūn
Oh God, all I see in him is a husk.
A heartless, wretched shell. a Monster!

Waliyyah

He's still your baby brother, and you know deep down
He really loves you like one. And you love *him*.
Yes, the caliphate has clouded him…
The power. The drink. The powerful drink. Lord…
But love, my child. There never was a divide,
however wide, that could not be bridged by it.
Speak to him.

al-Ma'mūn

I can't! I swear to God, I can't.

Waliyyah

You must.

al-Amīn calls from off stage

al-Amīn

Waliyyah! Waliyyah!

Waliyyah

Oh God Almighty. Remember what I said.

al-Ma'mūn kisses her forehead and both her hands, and she hurries off

al-Ma'mūn

Oh father, curse his hands!
How did you not foresee such travesty!
Even now he insults your noble name.
The House of Abbas, the bastion of righteousness–
now tossed in the throes of a drunken hack!
He did not even love you. *I* loved you!
All that I've done– every single thing–
I've done to make you proud. You were my all,
the only family I ever had to claim.
Zubayda. She… is no mother to me.
She loved you, yes, but she loved Muhammad more.
Many a night I often wonder still–
why did you choose to bereave me of *my* mother?
Was she just another concubine to you?
Was I simply a mistake that burdened you,
guilted you into taking sympathy?
Most of all, what compelled you to sell
the mother of your eldest child to a Byzantine?
Well, death can no longer hide your skeletons.
I fear that one may soon turn into the spectre
of malefaction, whose veil shall doom us all
to ruin. Oh God this place is some mad-house
and I… am numb. I..I feel nothing I…
I must retire. Tomorrow. Yes. Tomorrow
I will talk to the wazir. He was good
to father, God willing he'll lend an ear to me!

al-Ma'mūn exits stage right, al-Amīn, Zubayda enter stage left followed by Waliyyah

al-Amīn

Well they'll have to settle then, won't they.
Why on earth do these councilmen come to me
with all of this? Where's my treasurer,
I have one don't I? Send them to *him* for their pay.
I tell them where and whom to fight. That is all.
I'm not their damned banker.

Zubayda

And what about…

al-Amīn

What about what *mother*!? Yes I know
meet with him, council that, sign this
read that, have I no chance at all to think
or sleep or...

Zubayda

...drink? Right. Waliyyah! Come here.

Zubayda hands her an empty jug

more wine for your caliph.

Waliyyah turns to face al-Amin

Waliyyah

Muhammad, I think you should rest. You've had enough to drink tonight

Zubayda slaps Waliyyah hard, throws her to the ground, beats her

Zubayda

How dare you turn your back to me, slave?
You disobey me? Wretched thing!
He is not your son, he's your master,
as am I, and I swear to God Almighty
if you disrespect me one more time…

al-Ma'mūn rushes in stage right

al-Ma'mūn

Waliyyah! Zubayda stop!

al-Ma'mūn throws himself over Waliyyah, protecting her

Enough! What is wrong with you, both
of you!? That is it. I'm gathering my things,
Waliyyah and I are leaving tonight, she's coming

back to Marv with me…

al-Amīn
She's not going anywhere.

END SCENE

ACT I, SCENE III

Many years prior, during the time of Hārūn al-Rashīd. The two brothers as young adolescents, in a courtyard playing chess

al-Amīn

Tell me a story.

al-Ma'mūn

I have no story to tell brother.

al-Amīn

What a liar. Lying to your younger brother
again. Go on, tell me one that ever-
ambling teacher of ours recounts with unblinking
eyes and with such vigour. I seem to have
forgotten most of them. I get lost
and muddled in his winded spouts concerning

those dullard philosophers the both of you love
so much.

al-Ma'mūn
Do peripatetic intellectuals drunkenly
Greeking away at the soul and substance of man
while sitting at banquet tables too hungover
from the night before, who subsequently
rant lyrical, lamenting the qualities
of Love Divine only to stumble back
into a raging bacchanal with houri
boys not capture your eager mind, brother?
What a shame.

al-Amīn
Knowledge rears its head in many ways,
Ma'mun. You drink of the poets' mystic flagon.
I, dear brother, prefer a different aphrodisiac.

al-Ma'mūn
Rakishness is not a virtue, Muhammad.
The touch of a woman is knowledge of what erelong
decays like the dust beneath our feet.

al-Amīn
Why not live outside of books and breathe
of plebeian air? Why not sample life?

All you long for is to shrivel up
into a lonely raisin lost in thought
whose only joy in life is to ferment
and paralyse a host to a drunken stupor
of antiquated prehabilitations.
Go on then! Let me drink a dram of your heady
parables. Check.

al-Ma'mūn
Pick a topic.

al-Amīn
War.

al-Ma'mūn
Dark.

al-Amīn
What about… man's love. For war.

al-Ma'mūn
Let's see, what was it. Ah yes. One night…

al-Amīn
Check.

al-Ma'mūn

...in a lavish palace hall, Pharaoh held
a feast for his courtesans, all eyes upon
their gracious host. Amidst the revelry
a wandering vagrant came in and prostrated before
the Prince of Egypt. Pharaoh saw that he'd lost
an eye and blood dripped out from the empty socket.
"What happened to you old man?" Pharaoh asked.
"My lord, by trade I am a thief, and in
the moonless dark I aimed to rob a miserly
money-changer, but then I realised
I'd climbed into a weaver's shop and fell
onto the weaver's loom and lost this eye.
Now my lord, I ask that justice be passed
upon the weaver." So the weaver was summoned.
He raised his voice and it was then decreed
that one of the weaver's eyes should likewise be plucked.
The weaver accepted the charge and decreed the decision
just and that one of his eyes be plucked,
"though both my eyes," he said, "are required that I
may see both sides of the woven cloth."
"However, my neighbour the cobbler," the weaver con-
tinued, "requires neither eye to work his craft."
Pharaoh then sent for the cobbler and ruled that one
of his eyes be plucked, and justice was served.

al-Amīn

Ha! Check-mate.

al-Ma'mūn

Bravo Muhammad. That was most impressive.
With any luck, you'll be as astute and decisive
against the Byzantines when you become
caliph.

al-Amīn

You just wait and see my dear Ma'mun.
It is my opinion that every ruler has
the chance and the choice to avoid becoming
the pawn to be pushed, the knight to be bested and the king
to be crushed.

al-Ma'mūn

And the saviour queen?

al-Amīn

She has her uses. Explain to me this, Ma'mun.
The cobbler. In your story. What was his crime?

al-Ma'mūn

Innocence.

al-Amīn

Shocking. The plague of innocence in times of war.
Your parables are boring as they are hollow.
Pawns, they have no use for eyes, Ma'mun.
That is what makes them pawns.

al-Ma'mūn

Yes Muhammad. But let me ask you this
Which is more dangerous, a one-eyed pawn
or a fully-blind king?

al-Amīn smiles at his brother

al-Amīn

You will make a brilliant caliph someday.

al-Ma'mūn

I only aim to be the brilliant servant
of my future caliph, my brother, al-Amīn.
Here, I wanted to give you something.

al-Ma'mūn pulls out a fist-sized, spherical, golden music box with a square base

al-Amīn

What is it?

al-Ma'mūn
It's a music box. My mother - bless her heart -
she gave it to me when I was a little boy.
Not long before… I want you to have it.
It's from Byzantium.

Hands al-Amīn the music box. He opens it, music plays

al-Amīn
That melody…

al-Ma'mūn
Haunting, isn't it?

al-Amīn
It's beautiful.

al-Ma'mūn
It's all I have left of her.

al-Amīn
Thank you brother. I will cherish it.

Closes the music box

al-Amīn
Another game?

al-Ma'mūn
Always.

END SCENE

ACT II, SCENE I

Back to the present. The caliphal court, al-Amīn pacing pensively, with Zubayda and Waliyyah present

Zubayda

Dear, dear boy. You look awful!
You're letting all this business get to your head!

al-Amīn

What the hell do you mean 'this business'? This
is not business, this is anarchy!
When was running an empire considered business?
Is that the way you see all of this? My God
father must be rolling in his grave!

Zubayda

Those Byzantines are nothing but parasites,
Muhammad, they rear their heads, you snuff them out

wherever they flair, they'll just regroup and flair
back up again. It hasn't changed in decades!

al-Amīn
Byzantines, mother? Byzantines?!
It's my own people! Every day I hear
reports of cities pledging loyalty
to al-Ma'mun. I've practically lost every city
in Persia! Byzantines you say? They
are the last thing on my mind, I promise you that.

Zubayda
That insolent wretch of a man, this is treason!

al-Amīn
My ministers have been reporting for weeks
of riots along the borders of Khorasan,
that my brother's been funding his own defence forces,
rumors of alliances with Charlemagne
and his Christian armies...

Zubayda
That treacherous dog!

al-Amīn
That treacherous dog is my brother!

Zubayda
...who turns his back on you, appropriates
your forces, allies himself with infidels–
you and your father's lifelong enemies,
over what? That bitch of a slave of yours!

al-Amīn
Enough! This has nothing to do with her,
and if it did, it would be your fault!

Waliyyah covers her face, sobbing quietly

Don't you see? Ma'mun's power has been
consolidating for longer than I can remember,
without even trying! My people have elected
him as their new caliph, practically and frankly,
mother, I find it hard to blame them.

Zubayda
People do not elect their caliphs Muhammad,
Be vigilant! Be a man! You must crush them with
an iron fist!

al-Amīn
Get out! Get out! Now!

Fuming, Zubayda leaves the court

What is happening, Waliyyah? What have I done!?

al-Amīn falls to his knees, covering his face, Waliyyah still teary-eyed

Make it stop! Make this all go away!

gets up, faces and walks towards the audience, addressing them

Every hour passes bent against me!
In my chest, the crushing pain of bitter
destitution. I feel a thousand eyes
glaring at me, hidden in the shadows
and every shadow follows closely, cursing.
Light itself, that blessing! fails to rescue.
Each day anew announces multitudes
of demons that by the evenings only treble,
their nooses tighten and I against their grip
am impotent!

Looks up, addressing the heavens

Oh father what is this
unholy thing you left me with, this so-called
power, this soulless mantle of pure destruction?
What glory does power bring with it to mask

its ignobility? I am condemned!
Oh father what have you bestowed me with
that poisons from within this House of Abbas?
I never wanted any part of this!
It should have been Ma'mun, and I know you knew it too!
All I wanted was to be left alone,
to be free, unfettered from the annals of time!
Now… it is too late.

Sits on his throne, pours himself a cup of wine, stairs at it

I have defaced
our chapter of history beyond repair.
May God have mercy on my putrid soul.

As he downs his glass, Wazir bursts into the court, panting, carrying a letter

Wazir
My lord! My lord, a letter's come from Marv,
from the governorate.

al-Amīn
Not now Wazir, I wish to be alone!

Wazir
My caliph, Commander of the Faithful, it is urgent!

From your brother, governor al-Ma'mūn.

Wazir hands al-Amīn the letter

It's a list of demands. A-a-an ultimatum.

al-Amīn after reading it a while, crumbles it up, still holding it

al-Amīn
Wazir.

Wazir
My lord?

al-Amīn
Alert my councilmen immediately.
Tell them to bolster the city's siege defenses.
And prepare the army.

Wazir
Right away my lord.

Wazir hurries off. al-Amīn, pours another cup of wine, stairs at it, and after a while, gets up, throws it against a wall before exiting the stage. Waliyyah, alone in the court, addresses the audience

Waliyyah

Oh Baghdad, my Baghdad– the jewel, the envy of the world. Never has it seen a time as dark as this. Never has the House of Abbas been plagued by such internal conflict. Blood against blood, brother against brother. My two boys. The two lights of my life, now desperate in their attempts to extinguish the other. I bore witness to it, utterly powerless, trapped, peering out from the confines of the palace. al-Ma'mūn's armies from Persia besieged the city for over a year, barricading it, with no-one able to enter or leave its limits. So much life– innocent life– lost in the crossfire. But despite the year-long resistance, the city walls began to wear away from the endless barrage of al-Ma'mūn's siege engines. For many in the city, the weakening of al-Amin's resistance was a mercy from God. al-Ma'mūn's forces finally penetrated the city walls and entered the palace gates. All things, after all, must come to an end. Still, no-one dared imagine how that end– to a conflict of such fierce animosity– would unfold.

END SCENE

ACT II, SCENE II

al-Amīn stumbles into his palace bedroom, one way in, one way out, panicking

al-Amīn

God Almighty what is happening?
What have I done that so displeased you,
to leave me here, trapped in my own quarters?
Oh God, hear my cry, I'm begging you!
Save me from their wrath in this dire hour.
Do not leave me here alone to die,
defend these walls against these enemies, my enemies,
my brother's mercenaries!

turns to address the audience

Not a single man did I spare to fight
these rebels, these traitors who defy their own caliph.

They serve the man whom I loved all my life,
my kin, my own, now desperate to capture me
or worse! How could I not satisfy
his every whim? I gave him love, gave him
land, power and riches the world over.
Why bite the hand who fed you, or covet the throne
that served you? Now look at me! On the run
in my own home, surrounded on every side.
I feel... now... the full brunt of my failure–
to my people, my land, my house... my religion.
All has turned against me. I am nothing!
Fallen from the summit to the rank
of petty fugitive– a wanted man.
Maybe I should just come clean and turn
myself in, they may still grant me amnesty.
What in the hell do I have left to cling to
anyway? Ma'mun can have it all!
God Almighty, just let him spare my life!

Enter Wazir

Wazir
My caliph!

al-Amīn
Wazir! Have mercy, tell me something good,
anything!

Wazir
As it stands I'm afraid it's looking bleak.
The rebels have completely overrun the city.
My caliph, they are at your doorstep. Your guards
as we speak are struggling to repel them
from these perimeters. All I can do,
is assure you that they will fight to the death for you.

al-Amīn
Would they, Wazir?

Wazir
Of course they would. In that I have no doubt.
But you must bide your time wisely, Muhammad.
Prepare for the worst if it comes to pass.

Waliyyah runs into the room

Waliyyah
Muhammad!

al-Amīn
Waliyyah!

Waliyyah
Oh thank God, your safe.

al-Amīn
For how much longer, I'm afraid I do not know.

Waliyyah
I've been searching every room looking
for you. This was the first place I looked,
but you weren't here!

al-Amīn
Where is my mother, Waliyyah?

Waliyyah
I'm sorry, I couldn't find her anywhere!
She must be hiding somewhere in the palace.
Oh God, what are they going to do to us?
They've made it past the palace guards!

al-Amīn
Lord Almighty, I don't know Waliyyah.
It is not you they're after though, I swear.
They will not touch you, your return to Marv
was on the list of demands.

Waliyyah begins to weep

Waliyyah
Oh God, forgive me Muhammad I'm so sorry!

I did not mean to get between you
and Ma'mun, Oh God have mercy on my soul!
I feel I've destroyed this house, destroyed Baghdad!

al-Amīn
Waliyyah, stop, you've done nothing wrong,
you've done nothing! It is me! It is all me.
I failed you, and now... I must pay for my failure.

Waliyyah
No you don't Muhammad, there must be a way!
Escape! Leave Baghdad and don't come back.
I will disguise you.

al-Amīn
There's no point, Waliyyah. They will find us.

Waliyyah
I know a way, a-a-a passage, it leads out to
the Tigris. You can take a boat south
to Faisaliyyah, you'll be safe there.

al-Amīn
You're sure you can get me out?

Waliyyah
Yes, a million times yes, I swear!

al-Amīn
Then go Waliyyah. Get me some rags to wear.
Hurry.

Waliyyah runs out. al-Amīn picks up his brother's music box from his bedside, opens it, music plays, then closes it again.

Come with us, Wazir, we can go together.

Wazir
I'm afraid I can't. My place is here,
my caliph. All my life I've had the supreme
honour of serving the lords of this house
and I would die before I abandon her.
Her fortune shall be my fortune and her demise
shall be mine. But I will do my part to protect
her last sovereign, my commander of the faithful.
I have but one regret– that I could do nothing
to prevent this war.

al-Amīn
You've been good to us, Wazir. To father,
to me, even my brother. Whatever happens,
may God protect you and keep you.

al-Amīn reaches out to Wazir. Then as they embrace

each other, Wazir pulls out a dagger and stabs al-Amīn in the back. al-Amīn stumbles to his knees.

al-Amīn

You… why?

Wazir

I may not have prevented this war, but with God
as my witness, history will remember me
as the man who ended it.

al-Amīn looks up

al-Amīn

F-f-father… I… bear witness…

Wazir with his dagger delivers a final blow, al-Amīn falls dead

Wazir

Āmeen, Emīr al-Mu'mineen.

Waliyyah runs in with the rags, screams at the sight of al-Amīn, crying, races towards his body

Waliyyah

Muhammad! Muhammad! Wazir what have you done!?

Wazir

It's done Waliyyah. The war. It's over.

Waliyyah

Goddamn your wretched soul, you bastard, you traitor!

Wazir grabs the music box from beside al-Amīn, then grabs Waliyyah

Wazir

Waliyyah it's over! I'm taking you with me to Marv, to our new caliph, al-Ma'mun.

Waliyyah

No! Nooooo!

She screams hysterically. As she is dragged away, she looks back at the corpse, weeping

END SCENE

ACT II, SCENE III

al-Ma'mūn's court in Marv, Persia. Wazir knocks at the entrance

al-Ma'mūn

Please! Enter son of Adam.

Wazir

Your eminence.

al-Ma'mūn

Ah, Wazir!

Wazir

Peace be upon you.

al-Ma'mūn

And you old friend. I have to say,

I was not expecting you. Tell me,
what is the purpose of your visit, what news have you
for me? a message from my brother?

Wazir
No, your excellency.

al-Ma'mūn
So you escaped, did you? Defect? Speak freely,
Wazir.

Wazir
Neither, my lord. I've come by my own volition.
I've come bearing his excellency a gift.

Wazir opens the entrance, Waliyyah enters

Waliyyah
Ma'mun!

al-Ma'mūn
Waliyyah!

Run towards each other, embrace

Praise the Lord Almighty, my dearest Waliyyah,
How I've missed you!

Wazir
That is not all. I have another gift
to share with you, my lord. Or should I say,
my caliph.

al-Ma'mūn
What are you saying, Wazir?

Wazir
I came as soon as I could to tell you first hand.
The war– it's over. You are victorious.
Baghdad is yours, my caliph.

al-Ma'mūn
And what of my brother? Where is my brother, Wazir

Wazir
Al-Amīn has been… dispatched. I saw
to it personally. And Zubayda, the queen,
has been placed under house-arrest and awaits
your deliberation.

al-Ma'mūn
Is this true, Waliyyah?

Waliyyah
What he says is true, Ma'mun.

al-Ma'mūn gets up, begins pacing slowly

al-Ma'mūn
This news... is quite auspicious Wazir, is it not?

Wazir
It is my caliph. God's dominion is yours.

al-Ma'mūn
God's dominion. The caliphate. Auspicious
news indeed. I do not know which gift
supersedes the other. How do I
repay a man who offers the world itself?

Wazir
However my lord sees fit.

al-Ma'mūn chuckles

al-Ma'mūn
Yes.

Wazir
It is what God intended. What your father
intended. I swear on my life. Wait, I almost
forgot. My final gift to you.

Pulls out the music box, kneels. al-Ma'mūn walks towards him

I thought I'd return it to you, my caliph.

Still kneeling, hands al-Ma'mūn the music box. al-Ma'mūn opens it, music plays, then shuts it, stares at it, then suddenly starts beating Wazir's head with it

Waliyyah
Ma'mun! Stop!

Tries but fails to pull al-Ma'mūn away. al-Ma'mūn bludgeons Wazir to death, then drops the bloody music box

Oh God! You are all mad men, all
of you! What has happened… to my boys… Wazir….
That is it. I can't take anymore of this killing.
You've all turned to monsters! Well I've had
enough. I'm leaving, Ma'mun, and I'm not coming
back.

As she walks away, al-Ma'mūn grabs her arm, but she immediately jerks it away

Waliyyah
No, don't touch me!

al-Ma'mūn
Waliyyah! Please...don't go… don't leave me here alone. Waliyyah, please.

Waliyyah
Goodbye Ma'mun.

Waliyyah exits

al-Ma'mūn
Waliyyah! Waliyyah!

al-Ma'mūn begins to sob, covering his face. Eventually stops, picks up the music box, slowly walks back to his throne and sits down. After a while, opens the music box, stares at it for a while, then drops it by his side, music still playing, lighting turns off, stage goes dark, music plays a few seconds longer then ends on a cadence

FIN